IS TH
LIFE AFTER
HIGH SCHOOL?

A Musical

Book by
Jeffrey Kindley
Music and Lyrics by
Craig Carnelia

suggested by the book by

Ralph Keyes

SAMUEL FRENCH, INC.
25 WEST 45TH STREET   NEW YORK 10036
7623 SUNSET BOULEVARD   HOLLYWOOD 90046
LONDON   *TORONTO*

Important Advertising and Billing Requirements

The names of Jeffrey Kindley, Craig Carnelia and Ralph Keyes must receive credit in any and all advertising, publicity, and exploitation of the play for amateur and stock production. Their names must appear in all theatre programs, houseboards, billboards, advertisements, marquees, displays, posters, throwaways, circulars, announcements, and whenever and wherever the title of the play appears immediately following the title of the play. The names of Jeffrey Kindley and Craig Carnelia must be equal in size, type and prominence, and at least 50% of the size, type and prominence of the title type or the type accorded to the name of the play, or the stars, whichever is larger. The credit to Ralph Keyes shall be one-third of the size of the credit to Jeffrey Kindley and Craig Carnelia. No credits shall appear in type larger or more prominent than the credit to Jeffrey Kindley and Craig Carnelia except for the title of the play and stars who receive credit above the title of the play, and stars who receive credit above the title of the play, and provided further that stars, the director and the choreographer of any stock or amateur production shall be the only persons who may receive credit as large and as prominent as Jeffrey Kindley and Craig Carnelia. The billing shall be in the following form:

(Name of Producer)

presents

IS THERE LIFE AFTER HIGH SCHOOL?
Book by   Music and Lyrics by
JEFFREY KINDLEY   CRAIG CARNELIA
Suggested by the book by Ralph Keyes

In addition, the following credit must appear in a conspicuous place on the first page of credits in all programs:

"Produced on the Broadway Stage by
Clive Davis, Francois de Menil,
Harris Maslansky and Twentieth
Century Fox-Theatre Productions, Inc."

A final billing requirement is that credit be given to Bruce Coughlin as follows:

"Orchestrations by Bruce Coughlin"

This billing should be comparable in size as to the billing given to Ralph Keyes, and only need be included in those productions which use the 9-piece band arrangements (or some substantial part of those arrangements).

2

IS THERE LIFE AFTER HIGH SCHOOL? opened on May 7, 1982, at the Ethel Barrymore Theatre in New York City. It was produced by Clive Davis, Francois de Menil and Harris Maslansky, and Twentieth Century-Fox Theatre Productions. The production was staged by Robert Nigro. The set was designed by John Lee Beatty, the costumes by Carol Oditz, and the lighting by Beverly Emmons. Sound design was by Tom Morse. The musical direction and orchestrations were by Bruce Coughlin. The original cast was as follows:

WOMAN 1 .... *Alma Cuervo*
WOMAN 2 .... *Cynthia Carle*
WOMAN 3 .... *Maureen Silliman*
WOMAN 4 .... *Sandy Faison*
MAN 1 .... *Philip Hoffman*
MAN 2 .... *David Patrick Kelly*
MAN 3 .... *Raymond Baker*
MAN 4 .... *James Widdoes*
MAN 5 .... *Harry Groener*

PRODUCTION NOTES

There are nine actors in the cast: four women and five men. They are between the ages of 27 and 37 — which is to say, ten to twenty years beyond high school. Each of the actors portrays many different characters in the course of the play. They speak to the audience throughout, except where otherwise specified in the script.

The set is a composite of everyone's remembered high school, intended to evoke what Ralph Keyes calls "the hallways of your mind". In the New York production the set was a two-level pseudo-cinderblock structure in tones of institutional green and dull pink. The 9 piece band was situated upstage center on the second level. The balustrades, the light fixtures, the windows, the woodwork, the flooring — all brought back the quintessential American high school. A row of students' desks entered when needed on a palette Stage Right. Decorations for the prom in Act I and for the reunion in Act II were flown in to transform the basic set. It is quite possible to perform the play on a far less elaborate set, however. Even a bare stage will suffice if the production is staged imaginatively.

The actors wear basic street costumes (standard contemporary dress) which can be varied subtly to suggest changes of character. In some instances, as in the remembered fight between JERRY DOYLE and EDDIE RONDELLO in Act I or in the song "BEER", the formality of the clothes worn (business suits) heightens the contrast between past and present selves. In Act II, when the reunion sequence begins, the actors change into dressier outfits as they prepare to meet their classmates again.

MUSICAL NUMBERS

ACT I

ACT II

Is There Life After High School?

ACT ONE

AT RISE: *A school bell rings, and we see the entire cast standing in a TABLEAU Center Stage as if posing for a class picture. We hear a pre-recorded roll call — an echo of the past.*

TEACHER'S VOICE. Ackerman.
1ST STUDENT'S VOICE.   Here.
TEACHER'S VOICE. Alberts.
2ND STUDENT'S VOICE. Here.
TEACHER'S VOICE. Beckford.
3RD STUDENT'S VOICE. Here.
TEACHER'S VOICE. Berger.
4TH STUDENT'S VOICE. Here.
TEACHER'S VOICE. Cassidy.
5TH STUDENT'S VOICE. Here.
TEACHER'S VOICE. Davidson.
6TH STUDENT'S VOICE. Present!
TEACHER'S VOICE. Feinstein.
7TH STUDENT'S VOICE. Here.
TEACHER'S VOICE. Heissman.

(*The sound tape fades and music begins. WOMAN 1 steps out of the TABLEAU and speaks to the audience.*)

WOMAN 1. I've been out of school for fifteen years, and I still have total recall of my home-room attendance. Like my Latin teacher used to say, "If you learn it by heart as a teenager, it'll stay with you the rest of your life."

(*The others now begin to break out of the TABLEAU. MAN 1 begins singing "THE KID INSIDE".)*

Man 1.
THERE'S A KID INSIDE,
AND I HAVE HIM WITH ME ALWAYS.
　Woman 2.
THERE'S A KID INSIDE,
WALKING DOWN OLD HIGH SCHOOL HALLWAYS.
　Women 1 & 3, Men 2, 3, 4.
THERE'S A KID INSIDE,
　Woman 3.
AT A DESK,
　Woman 1 & Man 2.
AT A DANCE,
　Woman 2 & Man 3.
IN THE HALLS,
　Man 4.
IN THE SHOWERS.
　All Seven.
THERE'S A KID INSIDE,
　Man 1.
TO THIS VERY DAY.
　Man 5.
AND HE MAKES A TRY
FOR THE HIGH POP FLY
THAT I FUMBLED ONE SEPTEMBER.
　Woman 4.
AND SHE MAKES A FUSS
OVER SOME A-PLUS
THAT I SHOULDN'T STILL REMEMBER.
　All.
AND HE GOES ALONG
　5 Voices.
GETTING HURT,
　4 Voices.
GETTING MAD,
　All.
FIGHTING FIGHTS THAT ARE OVER.
AND UNLESS I'M STRONG,
ALL MY SENSES ARE CARRIED AWAY.
　Woman 3.
I CAN FEEL JOHN'S HAND
　Man 5.
(MY TREMBLING HAND)

WOMAN 3.
ON MY OLD ANGORA SWEATER.
MAN 1.
I CAN HEAR MY BAND,
MAN 3.
(THAT AWFUL BAND)
MAN 1.
ONLY NOW IT SOUNDS MUCH BETTER.
ALL BUT MAN 2.
I CAN SEE THE KID
MAN 2.
(THE KID I USED TO BE)
3 VOICES.
ON THE STAGE,
2 VOICES.
ON THE FIELD,
4 VOICES.
ON THE LUNCH LINE.
7 VOICES.
I CAN FEEL HIM TUGGING AT ME.
ALL.
I CAN HEAR HIM SAY:

ALWAYS REMEMBER.
NEVER FORGET.
ALWAYS REMEMBER.
NEVER FORGET.
ALWAYS REMEMBER
MAN 2.
CHOOSING SIDES.
ALL.
NEVER FORGET
WOMAN 2 & MAN 5.
DANCING IN THE GYM.
ALL.
ALWAYS REMEMBER
WOMAN 3.
SAYING SOMETHING DUMB.
ALL.
NEVER FORGET
WOMAN 4 & MAN 1.
BEING CHEERED BY THE CROWD.

ALL.
ALWAYS REMEMBER
  4 VOICES.
THE FACES, THE NAMES.
  ALL.
NEVER FORGET
  5 VOICES.
WHO WAS POPULAR AND WHO WAS NOT.
  ALL.
REMEMBER THE DATES,
AND THE LOVES, AND THE HATES, AND THE GAMES.
  MEN.
AND WHEN I THINK I FORGOT:
  ALL.
THERE'S A KID INSIDE
KEEPING TRACK, KEEPING SCORE,
LIKE IT'S ALL STILL IMPORTANT.

THERE'S A KID INSIDE.
EVERY TIME I THINK I DON'T CARE
I BLINK AND HE'S THERE AGAIN.

HE'S THERE AGAIN.
FIGHTING ANCIENT WRONGS,
HUMMING OLD HIT SONGS IN MY HEAD.
SINGING "COME ALONG, COME ALONG,
COME ALONG FOR THE RIDE."
TO A TIME AND PLACE
I COULD NOT FORGET IF I TRIED.

ALWAYS REMEMBER

  MAN 4. Melanie Abbott.
  ALL BUT MAN 4.
NEVER FORGET
  MAN 1. Amo, amas, amat.
  ALL BUT MAN 1.
ALWAYS REMEMBER
  WOMAN 4. It was blue chiffon.
  ALL BUT WOMAN 4.
NEVER FORGET

(*music continues under*)

MAN 5. My S.A.T. scores.

MAN 2. Then Ellen said, "You won! You're the new class president!"

WOMAN 4. Blue chiffon with pink rosebuds.

WOMAN 1. When I think about high school . . . Oh, God. I don't wanna think about it.

MAN 3. Harriman High.

WOMAN 3. St. Agnes.

WOMAN 2. Polytech.

MAN 4. Grover Cleveland Memorial High School.

MAN 1. It's like it never ended. I mean, what the hell was I doing last night dreaming about Richard Delavecchio?

WOMAN 3. She wasn't any better than I was, so why'd she get to be cheerleader?

MAN 5. My high jump record still stands at Oceanside.

WOMAN 3. I could do the splits, and she couldn't!

MAN 4. Screw them! Didn't want to sit at their table anyway.

MAN 2.

THERE HE GOES AGAIN

MAN 3. We came *this close* to taking State.

ALL.

THERE HE / SHE GOES AGAIN

WOMAN 1. Charlie! Charlie Rogers!

ALL.

AND I NEVER KNOW

WHEN THE BREEZE'LL BLOW

WITH A RUSH OF OLD SENSATIONS.

WHY THE KID SHOULD WAKE,

AND MY HEART SHOULD ACHE

EVERY TIME I SMELL CARNATIONS.

SOMETHING RINGS A BELL.

4 VOICES.

(ANYTHING AT ALL)

ALL.

ALL IT TAKES IS THE SLAM OF A LOCKER,

OR THE SWITCH FROM SUMMER TO FALL.

A CHANGE OF SEASON

SEEMS BARELY REASON, BUT

WOMEN.	MEN.
THERE AGAIN	THERE HE GOES AGAIN,
SHE'S THERE AGAIN;	HUMMIN' HIS SONGS.

ALL.
FIGHTING ANCIENT WRONGS,
HUMMING OLD HIT SONGS IN MY HEAD.
SINGING "COME ALONG, COME ALONG.
COME ALONG FOR THE RIDE."
    THERE'S A KID INSIDE.
TO A TIME AND PLACE
I COULD NOT FORGET IF I TRIED.
    THERE'S A KID INSIDE.
THERE HE GOES AGAIN.
    THERE AGAIN.
HUMMIN' HIS SONGS.
    THERE'S A KID INSIDE.
HE'S THERE AGAIN,
    THERE AGAIN.
THERE'S A KID INSIDE.

*   *   *

(*After applause the music begins again softly.*)

ALL BUT MAN 2.
ALWAYS REMEMBER
    MAN 2. Twelve to the right, twenty-one to the left, four to the right. (*HE exits.*)
    ALL BUT MAN 1 & WOMAN 2. (*as they exit, except for WOMAN 3*)
ALWAYS REMEMBER
    MAN 1. What I wish is that I could live it all again. (*HE exits.*)
    WOMAN 2. I wish I'd never had to live through it in the first place. (*SHE exits. WOMAN 3 is left alone on stage.*)
    ELLEN CLARK (WOMAN 3). I don't want to sound like a fanatic or anything, but Mary Jo Drennan ruined my senior yearbook, and I'll never forgive her for it. On the very first page of the book she wrote, "Roses are red, Violets are blue. If I had your breath, I'd go live in a zoo." She wrote this with a green felt-tip pen right on top of the picture of our school. After I read what she wrote, I never let anyone else sign my book again, or even look at it. I just stuck it away in an old bookcase at home. And then last week the mailman handed me this package . . . My mother sent me the yearbook because she thought I should have it to show my kids. At first I was going to hide it, but I realized that sooner or later it'd come up again, and something had to be

done about it. So . . . I bought a green felt-tip pen and practiced imitating Mary Jo's handwriting, and then right after her poem I wrote, in big letters, "HA, HA — JUST KIDDING." What embarrasses me most isn't what she wrote in my book. It's that I'm 28 years old and I still care.

(*SHE exits as MAN 5 enters and sings "THINGS I LEARNED IN HIGH SCHOOL" in an empty classroom. In the New York production the classroom, which contained a teacher's desk and a row of student desks, emerged on a mobile platform Up Center.*)

MAN 5.
I LEARNED TO COUNT TO TEN IN FRENCH.
I LEARNED TO CUT A FROG IN TWO.
I LEARNED THAT SHOWING HOW YOU FEEL
CAN BE A DEADLY THING TO DO.

AND THE THINGS I LEARNED IN HIGH SCHOOL
I CARRY WITH ME STILL.
THE LESSONS TAUGHT,
THE STUFF I THOUGHT,
THE JUNK I HEARD
AND THE CRAP I BOUGHT.
THE THINGS I LEARNED IN HIGH SCHOOL,
THE PARTS I LEARNED TO PLAY,
HAVE MADE ME WHAT I AM TODAY.

I LEARNED THE HISTORY OF THE WORLD.
I LEARNED THAT SOMETHING EQUALS "PI".
I LEARNED THAT GIVING UP IS FINE
AS LONG AS NO ONE SAW YOU TRY.

AND THE THINGS I LEARNED IN HIGH SCHOOL
HAVE BEEN THERE EVER SINCE.
THE FEELINGS TAUGHT,
THE HABITS CAUGHT,
THE HOPES I HELD
AND THE FEARS I FOUGHT.
THE THINGS I LEARNED IN HIGH SCHOOL
HAVE STUCK ALONG THE WAY,
AND MADE ME WHAT I AM . . .

THANKS A LOT.
THANKS A LOT
FOR ALL THE LESSONS I LEARNED.
I PICKED IT UP,
TOOK IT IN,
GOT IT DOWN ON THE SPOT.
THANKS A LOT.
THANKS A LOT,
TO ALL THE PARTIES CONCERNED,
FOR THE GREAT, WELL-ROUNDED
PUBLIC EDUCATION I GOT.

I LEARNED A LOT O' THINGS
A PERSON MIGHT BE BETTER NOT TO KNOW.
A LOT O' JUNK I
SHOULD'VE GOTTEN RID OF LONG AGO.
I LEARNED A LOT OF FACTS
THAT ARE NO LONGER EVEN SO.

BUT THE THINGS I LEARNED IN HIGH SCHOOL
ARE WITH ME ALL THE SAME.
IN HOW I THINK
AND HOW I SPEAK.
IN WHERE I'M STRONG
AND WHERE I'M WEAK.
THE PLAYING CUTE,
THE ACTING TOUGH,
THE NAGGING DOUBTS,
AND ENOUGH'S ENOUGH.

THE THINGS I LEARNED IN HIGH SCHOOL
CANNOT BE WISHED AWAY.
THEY MADE ME WHAT I AM TODAY.

*   *   *

(*After the song we see MAN 3, who is holding a yearbook.*)

MAN 3. I decided the best way to deal with high school was to get rid of all the evidence. For starters, there's the good ol' Harper High yearbook. (*HE rips out a page, wads it up, and tosses it over his shoulder.*) I'm telling you, this is a hell of a lot cheaper than therapy. (*HE exits and MAN 1 enters with a yearbook.*)

HARVEY BELLERBY (MAN 1). Here's a picture of Monica Ormus: the most popular girl at Yarborough High. And here's me: Harvey Bellerby, co-chairman of the Logarithm League. Just before final exam in Senior Algebra, Monica Ormus spoke to me for the first time ever. She asked me to cheat for her. What she wanted me to do was write out the answers on a piece of paper and let it fall to the floor. Then she'd drop a pencil, reach over to pick it up, and pick up the answers, too. If I did, she said she'd let me take her out sometime. This was my one chance, and I only had a second to decide. I was in pain—actual pain! I told her I couldn't. I didn't say "it's wrong" or anything; I just said I couldn't. From that moment on, she never spoke to me again. Two years out of school I got stoned one night, and before I knew what I was doing I called her up. Oh, Jesus. I said, "This is Harvey Bellerby." She said, "Who?" I said, "Harvey Bellerby, from Y.H.S." "Oh," she said. "What do *you* want?" I should've hung up, but I didn't. What I said was, "Well, Monica . . . I just want to tell you I've changed my mind." (*Five people at school desks sing "SECOND THOUGHTS".*)
ALL.
SECOND THOUGHTS . . .
SECOND THOUGHTS ABOUT . . .
MAN 3.
SECOND THOUGHTS ABOUT THE FRIEND I SNUBBED.
WOMAN 3.
SECOND THOUGHTS ABOUT THE SPEECH I FLUBBED.
MAN 4.
SECOND THOUGHTS ABOUT A CREEP NAMED TOD.
MAN 2.
SECOND THOUGHTS ABOUT DENISE. OH, GOD.
WOMAN 4.
SECOND THOUGHTS ABOUT THE FIGHT I SHOULD'VE WON.
ALL FIVE.
SECOND THOUGHTS OF WHAT I MIGHT
HAVE SAID AND DONE
MAN 2.
WHILE THE CHANCE WAS MINE.
WOMAN 4.
IF I'D ONLY FOUND THE WORDS THAT NIGHT.
MAN 4.
IF I'D ONLY HAD THE GUTS TO FIGHT.

Woman 3.
IF I'D ONLY CHECKED THE MIKE, WHO KNOWS?
  Man 3.
IF I'D ONLY CALLED HIM BACK, JUST SUPPOSE.
  Man 2.
IF I'D GOTTEN IN HER PANTS, THERE AND THEN.
  All Five.
IF I ONLY HAD THE CHANCE,
'F I ONLY HAD THE CHANCE AGAIN.

BUT SCHOOL IS OUT.
IT'S NOTHIN' I
CAN DO A THING ABOUT.
THE GAME IS OVER,
AND THERE AIN'T A DOUBT.
THE SCORE IS FINAL;
WHERE WE STOOD
IS WHERE WE STAND.

TIME TICKS ON,
AND FINDS YOU TALKIN' TO YOURSELF
IN GROWN-UP LAND.
THE CHANCE IS GONE.
I CAN'T BELIEVE I LET IT SLIP
RIGHT THROUGH MY HAND.

IF I KNEW THEN
WHAT I KNOW NOW:
WHAT I WOULD'VE SAID WAS . . .

  Man 3.
HEY, BILLYO,
I'M SORRY ABOUT BEFORE.
I'M SORRY I MADE YOU SORE.
YOU'RE STILL MY BEST FRIEND, OKAY?
I'M SUCH A JERK ANYWAY,
FORGIVE ME ABOUT TODAY.
  All But Man 3.
WHAT I WOULD'VE DONE WAS . . .
  Woman 3.
PUSH THE MIKE ASIDE.
GET MY TONGUE UNTIED.

KNOCK 'EM OFF THEIR FEET,
AND WATCH MY LANDSLIDE SLIDE.
THEY WOULDA GONE:
"YAAAAY JUDY!"
"YAAAAY JUDY!"
  ALL BUT WOMAN 3.
WHAT I SHOULDA SAID WAS . . .
  MAN 4.
IF - YOU - DUNK - ME -
EVER - A - GAIN - I'LL -
BUST YOUR FRIGGIN' HEAD, TOD.
GOD, THAT WOULD HAVE BEEN BEAUTIFUL.
IT WOULD HAVE BEEN . . .
  WOMAN 4.
MARGUERITE TOLD ME
YOU WERE T'D BECAUSE
YOU WERE CONVINCED
I GOT THE LEAD BECAUSE
BECKER WOULD NEVER
"BREAK THE HEART OF HIS PET."
HAH!
I GOT THE PART
'CAUSE I'M BETTER THAN YOU.
IT WOULD HAVE BEEN BEAUTIFUL.
  ALL BUT WOMAN 4.
IT WOULD HAVE BEEN BEAUTIFUL.
  MAN 2.
GIVE HER WHAT SHE WANTED.
I SHOULDA KNOWN ENOUGH TO
GIVE HER WHAT SHE WANTED.
SHE SAID IT WAS SAFE.
"THE SAFEST TIME" SHE SAID.
SAFE!
I DIDN'T KNOW WHAT SHE MEANT.
SO THAT WAS THE WAY IT WENT.
IF I ONLY WAS . . .
  ALL.
IF I ONLY WAS
HALF AS GOOD IN HIGH SCHOOL
AS I AM IN MY SECOND THOUGHTS.
HALF AS GOOD IN HIGH SCHOOL
AS I AM . . .

WHAT I WOULDA DONE/SAID WAS . . .
WHAT I SHOULDA DONE/SAID WAS . . .

(*All five sing the following parts simultaneously.*)

MAN 3.
HEY, BILLYO,
I'M SORRY ABOUT BEFORE.
I'M SORRY I MADE YOU SORE.
YOU'RE STILL MY BEST FRIEND, OKAY?
I'M SUCH A JERK ANYWAY,
FORGIVE ME ABOUT TODAY.
OKAY?
   WOMAN 3.
PUSH THE MIKE ASIDE.
GET MY TONGUE UNTIED.
KNOCK 'EM OFF THEIR FEET,
AND WATCH MY LANDSLIDE SLIDE.
THEY WOULDA GONE:
"YAAAAY JUDY!"
"YAAAAY JUDY!"
   MAN 4.
IF - YOU - DUNK - ME -
EVER - A - GAIN - I'LL -
BUST YOUR FRIGGIN' HEAD, TOD.
GOD, THAT WOULD HAVE BEEN BEAUTIFUL.
IT WOULD HAVE BEEN BEAUTIFUL.
   WOMAN 4.
MARGUERITE TOLD ME
YOU WERE T'D BECAUSE
YOU WERE CONVINCED
I GOT THE LEAD BECAUSE
BECKER WOULD NEVER
"BREAK THE HEART OF HIS PET."
HAH!
I GOT THE PART
'CAUSE I'M BETTER THAN YOU.
IT WOULD HAVE BEEN BEAUTIFUL.
   MAN 2.
GIVE HER WHAT SHE WANTED.
I SHOULDA KNOWN ENOUGH TO
GIVE HER WHAT SHE WANTED.

SHE SAID IT WAS SAFE.
"THE SAFEST TIME" SHE SAID.
SAFE!
I DIDN'T KNOW WHAT SHE MEANT.
SO THAT WAS THE WAY IT WENT.
   ALL.
IF I ONLY WAS
HALF AS GOOD IN HIGH SCHOOL
AS I AM IN MY SECOND THOUGHTS.
HALF AS GOOD IN HIGH SCHOOL
AS I AM IN MY SECOND THOUGHTS.

*   *   *

(*After applause*:)

   ALL.
WHAT I SHOULDA DONE/SAID WAS . . .

(*THEY all exit while singing the five simultaneous parts. The singing fades as WOMAN 2 enters.*)

MAIDA VINER (WOMAN 2). We had something at my school called Daisy Days, which was the last week of the year, and there was always a Daisy Princess chosen from all the senior girls. On a certain day in June, every single one of us had to walk across the auditorium stage in front of everybody and say our names into the microphone. This was supposed to be another example of Democracy In Action. The teachers would write down the names of the six prettiest girls, and then we'd all get to vote on them for Daisy Princess. That way nobody was overlooked. I still remember exactly what I wore on Elimination Day. I imagine we all do. What I remember best, though, is Nancy Dugan. She was the tallest girl in our class—taller than most of the boys, even. While the rest of us paraded across that stage and tried to smile as we said our names, she had the guts to go out there and say, "My name is Nancy Dugan, and I decline the nomination." (*Other actors enter one by one.*)
   MAN 1. I was voted best public speaker.
   WOMAN 1. I was voted friendliest.
   MAN 3. I was voted Student Council president.
   WOMAN 4. I was voted best dancer.

MAN 5. I'm the one who tallied the votes.

MAN 2. I didn't win any big awards or prizes. I know winning was the name of the game in high school, and if you couldn't point to some kind of trophy you weren't really anybody. Still, there was one time during a track meet when there were about six guys out in front of me and somebody in the crowd called out my name.

MAN 5. (*to MAN 2*) Come on, Sammy! You can do it, Sammy!

MAN 2. I only took third that day, but just hearing that guy yell my name has gotta be one of the best moments in my whole life. (*music cue*)

WOMAN 3. I was standing on the third step of the north stair-case—I even remember the step, that's how important it was—when Jack Soloway told me he thought I was sexy. We both blushed, and then I had to run to my next class, and I spent the whole period writing the word SEXY over and over in my note-book. It was the most thrilling thing that had ever, ever happened to me. I remember thinking I could die happy now. No matter what happened to me ever again, I could always tell my-self, "Jack Soloway said I was sexy." (*music cue*)

MAN 4. Once when I was cleaning out my wallet I decided to throw away a snapshot of my high school girlfriend. Who needs that kinda thing, right? Imagine me at 3 a.m., down on my hands and knees in the garage, sifting through the contents of the garbage can. Now imagine my wife asking me what I'm do-ing. (*Music begins. WOMAN 1 sings "NOTHING REALLY HAPPENED".*)

WOMAN 1.

HE ASKED ME OVER TO HIS HOUSE.

I WORE SUZANNE'S EMBROIDERED BLOUSE.

I STILL REMEMBER THAT NIGHT,

AND NOTHING REALLY EVEN HAPPENED.

WOMAN 2.

WE TALKED SOME TRUTH; WE TOLD SOME LIES.

WOMAN 3.

HE PUSHED THE HAIR AWAY FROM MY EYES.

WOMAN 4.

IT FELT SO DANGEROUS THEN,

WOMEN 1 & 4.

AND NOTHING REALLY EVEN HAPPENED.

ALL FOUR.

FUNNY, THE THINGS YOU THINK ABOUT.

FUNNY, THE THINGS YOU DON'T.
FUNNY, THE THINGS THAT FADE AWAY.
FUNNY, THE THINGS THAT WON'T.
  WOMAN 1.
THE GIRL I TRIED SO HARD TO HIDE.
  WOMEN 1 & 3.
THE WOMAN WAKING UP INSIDE.
  WOMEN 1, 2 & 3.
THE WAY I PICTURED HIS BED.
  ALL FOUR.
THE SCENES I SAW IN MY HEAD.

WONDER IF I SHOULD WRITE HIM.
WONDER IF I SHOULD CALL.
WONDER IF HE'D REMEMBER AT ALL.
I WONDER IF HE'D REMEMBER AT ALL.
  WOMAN 1.
A MILLION YEARS AGO TONIGHT
THE T.V. GLOWED IN BLACK AND WHITE.
  ALL FOUR.
AND I REMEMBER THAT GIRL;
  WOMAN 1, 2 & 3.
THAT GIRL ALONE WITH THAT BOY.
  WOMEN 1 & 2.
AND I REMEMBER THAT NIGHT;
  WOMAN 1.
THAT NIGHT WHEN NOTHING REALLY HAPPENED.

* * *

(*JERRY DOYLE, dressed in a business suit and carrying a brief-
    case, enters* S.L. *He puts down the briefcase.*)

JERRY DOYLE (MAN 3). Just picture this: it's 3:15 and everybody from the whole school knows what's gonna happen.
There're like a hundred kids out back in the parking lot just
waiting to see me cream Eddie Rondello. The tension is terrific,
'cause like everybody knows it's him or me, y'understand? I say
to him, "Okay, asshole—you ready?"

(*EDDIE RONDELLO enters* S.R., *speaking. HE also is wearing
    a business suit and puts down his briefcase.*)

EDDIE RONDELLO (MAN 5). . . . and I say, "You bet I am, you chicken-shit mick."

JERRY DOYLE. So I take off my shirt, see, and he takes off his.

EDDIE RONDELLO. Timmy said he'd referee, but where's Timmy? Nobody knows. So I say, "Screw the referee. Let's get on with it." Kids start backin' away all of a sudden, and I come at Doyle like crazy. My first punch is a beauty. Whammo! There's like this big roar from the crowd, and I'm feelin' good, y'know? Really good.

JERRY DOYLE. First I let him think he's got me. He goes punchin' away like the stupid wop he is, usin' up all his energy in the first two minutes. I go "Unnh! Uhhn! — lettin' on like he's really givin' it to me. An' all the time I'm thinkin', "That's it, Eddie — just wear yourself out." In two minutes he's like all done, an' except for the fact I got like blood comin' outa my ear, I'm fresh as a daisy.

EDDIE RONDELLO. Some girl starts screamin' 'cause she sees I clipped him on the ear, and he's kinda staggerin' around with all this blood all over him. She starts screamin' "Stop it! Stop it! Stop it!" an' that's when I made my big mistake. She yells, "You're murdering him!" and in like a split-second I turn away and then Doyle grabs me by the knees and topples me over on the black-top and starts poundin' me.

JERRY DOYLE. And I go like Bam! Bam! Bam! Bam! Ya give? Ya give? Ya give?

EDDIE RONDELLO. If she hadn't've made me turn away . . .

JERRY DOYLE. What are you? Say it! What are you?

EDDIE RONDELLO. Doyle was good. I gotta give 'im that.

JERRY DOYLE. (*after a pause*) Then I got scared all of a sudden 'cause I can see he's unconscious. The rest is kind of a blur. Patsy ran up and put her arms around me, I know that, and then Eddie opened his eyes and I could see he was okay. I mean, thank God. I coulda killed him.

EDDIE RONDELLO. I never said I give, that's the thing. I wouldn't. I think he respected me for that.

JERRY DOYLE. After the fight, o' course, I was like a king!

EDDIE RONDELLO. I coulda beat him, though. I coulda beat him. He knew that, too. (*Picking up their briefcases, they see each other for the first time.*)

JERRY DOYLE. (*slowly*) Hey . . . Eddie?

EDDIE RONDELLO. (*apprehensive, but pleased*) Jerry Doyle?

JERRY DOYLE. (*crossing to shake his hand*) Long time no see, fella.

EDDIE RONDELLO. (*while shaking hands—equally friendly*) Long time no see.

(*THEY walk off together. Music begins and crepe-paper decorations descend as a couple (WOMAN 3 and MAN 2) enter slow-dancing in prom attire. THEY represent an image of the past—a visible flashback to the senior prom. As THEY dance WOMAN 2 enters and watches them from a distance. (See piano-vocal score for cues.)*)

WOMAN 2. He looked so handsome, so . . . I don't know. Just the way I'd hoped, I guess. Not like a boy all dressed up in formal clothes. Like a man.

(*MAN 1 enters and watches the couple dancing.*)

MAN 1. It was the last time I saw her—the last good time—before college. We had a fight afterwards about something. But that night was beautiful, really beautiful. (*MAN 3 also looks on.*)

MAN 3. Mary Ann and I didn't go to the prom, but sometimes I wish we had. She said she'd rather just stay home and talk, because the prom was only a chance for the rich kids to show off and she thought it was stupid. That was the night Mary Ann got pregnant. She still says she's glad we didn't go, and I say, "Yeah, me too." High school ended real fast, y'know? Right now it seems like light years away.

(*The music changes to a ghostly interlude in which the dancers move toward and around the speakers and look at them. The music then shifts back and the couple begins slow-dancing again.*)

WOMAN 2. It really *was* the happiest night of my life. Don't get me wrong—I'm not complaining or anything. I just know that nothing is ever gonna be as wonderful and scary and . . . and romantic as the Senior Prom.

(*The couple keeps dancing until WOMAN 4 appears. The music stops abruptly as SHE speaks.*)

WOMAN 4. At my school the prom had to be cancelled because

of a bomb scare. I recommended that this be made an annual tradition. (*Lights out on WOMAN 4 and all the others.*)

* * *

(*MAN 4 enters, extremely agitated, and speaks to the audience.*)

JIM WANAMAKER (MAN 4). I had a dream last night where someone found out I never took these courses that were necessary for graduation, and I had to go back to school to make up the work. I sat down at a desk which was way too small for me, but nobody else in the classroom seemed to notice that I was any different from them. Then Mrs. Delaney—my American Problems teacher—hands out these test booklets, and I look at the cover and someone has drawn obscene pictures all over it. I don't know what to do. Should I tell Mrs. Delaney, and call attention to myself, or should I just ignore the pictures?—in which case she'll probably think *I* drew them. The pictures are in pencil, see, so I start to erase them. All of these little breasts and penises and stick-people doing horrible things to each other. But as soon as I get one part erased, I notice another one—and another. Finally the bell rings and Mrs. Delaney starts collecting the booklets and I realize I never even opened mine. I don't even know what the test was about. And what's worse, all the pictures are still there. I start tearing up the booklet like crazy and sticking pieces of it in my mouth, trying to chew it all up and swallow it before she gets to me. Then she's standing over me and she says, "Where's your booklet, James? What have you done with it?" That's as far as it went. I woke up in a cold sweat. I'd wanted to say, "I ate it, you bitch! I ate it!"—but I never talked back to Mrs. Delaney in my life.

(*HE exits as a flagbearer (MAN 1) enters to parade drumming. WOMEN 1, 2 and 4, and MEN 2 and 5 enter and stand in a row, holding their hands over their hearts. THEY recite the Pledge of Allegiance as if it were a round.*)

WOMEN 1, 2 & 4 and MEN 2 & 5. I pledge allegiance to the flag of the United States of America, and to the republic for which it stands. One nation, indivisible, with liberty and justice for all.
   WOMAN 4. Once upon a time I believed that you could cover up your pimples with Clearasil and nobody would know they were there.

MAN 5. I believed that trigonometry was gonna come in handy someday.

WOMAN 1. I believed that people who violated the dress code were born troublemakers and deserved whatever punishment they got.

MAN 2. When I was a sophomore, I believed in the honor system. When I was a junior, I believed in getting into college.

WOMAN 2. I believed that a woman's virginity is a pearl of great price. I believed that boys lost their respect for a girl if she didn't tell them when to stop. Still, when Jerry Geller was going off to Panama as an exchange student, and I really wanted him to know the way I felt about him, and he was so goodlooking and sweet and kind of shy, and he said if we both wanted to, it couldn't be wrong . . . Well, I decided I believed in Jerry Geller. (*The flagbearer and the five people who have spoken all exit simultaneously as music begins.*)

(*MAN 3 enters and begins singing "BEER".*)

MAN 3.
USED TO BE, ON A SATURDAY NIGHT,
MY TWO BUDDIES 'N ME, WE'D GET HIGH AS A KITE.
AND I'M TELLIN' YA WE WERE A HELL OF A SIGHT—
DRUNK AS A SKUNK IN MAY.

(*MAN 2 appears in a separate area of the stage.*)

MEN 2 & 3.
IT NEVER TOOK A LOT, JUST A SIX-PACK O' BEER.
BUT IT WORKED IN A SHOT, PUT US RIGHT ON OUR
   EAR.
AND THE TALK IT WAS NOT WHAT YOU'RE LIKELY
   TO HEAR
   MAN 3.
DOWN AT THE P. T. FUCKIN' A.

(*MAN 5 appears, also in a separate area.*)

MEN 2, 3 & 5.
MAN OH MAN, WE WERE SOMETHIN' TO SEE.
ON A HALF OF A CAN WE WERE GONE AS COULD BE.
   MAN 3.
WE WERE MADE IN JAPAN, MY TWO BUDDIES 'N ME—

MEN 2, 3 & 5.
DRINKIN' THE NIGHT AWAY.

(*Flashback: THEY are now together in the past as THEY sing a drunken "La La" verse. Their animated activity is a sharp contrast to their stillness in the present. Back in the present, MAN 3 sings. MEN 2 and 5 remain in the past in a freeze.*)

MAN 3.
NOW I'M HALFWAY THROUGH MY 32ND YEAR,
AND I STILL GET THIRSTY FOR A CAN OF BEER.
BUT I DON'T GO CRAZY LIKE A KID.
DON'T GO BANANAS THE WAY WE DID.

(*MEN 2 and 5 come to life for one riotous moment, then freeze again.*)

MAN 3.
I CAN DRINK ALL NIGHT BEFORE IT EVEN SHOWS.
NOW WHEN I GET LOADED NO ONE EVER KNOWS.
ONLY TROUBLE IS IT DOESN'T FEEL
LIKE IT USED TO FEEL.

(*Flashback: THEY come together for a second "La La" verse, which builds this time to an extended drunken dance. Back in the present, but still together, THEY sing:*)

MAN 3.
BUT IT DOESN'T FEEL,
  MAN 5.
NO, IT DOESN'T FEEL,
  MAN 2.
LIKE IT USED TO FEEL.

(*The three men stand frozen for a moment with their arms around each other's shoulders, as if in a snapshot, then break apart.*)

ALL.
TAKE ME BACK TO THOSE SATURDAY NIGHTS.
I'M TELLIN' YA, JACK, IF THEY HAD ANY FLIGHTS
I WOULD FLY—

Man 3.
TO GET TO WHERE MY LIFE WAS EASY AGAIN.
    Men 2 & 5.
I WOULD FLY—
    Man 3.
TO FEEL A FEELIN' THAT WAS TEN OUT O' TEN.
    Men 2 & 5.
I WOULD FLY—
    All.
TO BUY THE BEER AND MEET MY BUDDIES AND THEN
(*coming together again*)
OPEN A CAN AND CHUG A LUG A LUG AWAY,
(*in snapshot grouping*)
AND GET BOMBED OUT OF MY MIND!

* * *

(*After applause the "BEER" vamp plays as the three men exit
    and WOMAN 1 enters.*)

ROXANNE PRENDERGAST (WOMAN 1). What I remember most
about high school is my mother telling me not to worry that
nobody ever asked me out. I was a late bloomer, she said. And I
thought, "What if I never bloom?" And then one day in the spring
of my junior year, Ricky Dalton, who was captain of the swim-
ming team and used to sing solos with the glee club, came up to
me in the hall and asked if he could go out with me on Saturday
night and I said yes. I was so happy and nervous and excited.
And then . . . well, the very next morning I found out why he
asked me. I got a pink slip in home-room, which meant that I
had to go see the girls' vice-principal. I'd never gotten a pink slip
before, and I used to think that people who got them were in
deep trouble. I felt really sick to my stomach, even though I
knew I hadn't been doing anything bad, and when third period
came I went to the office. And Miss Haskell said . . . she said
there was something written about me in one of the boys' lava-
tories, and was it true? I started to cry, and I felt so sick I
couldn't even talk and Miss Haskell just kept saying "Is it true?"
"Is it true?" "Is it true?" Finally I said no it wasn't, and she said
that was all right then, but if it ever happened again I'd have to
be put on probation. And I said . . . I said I understood, and I
thanked her. I *thanked* her. But anyway . . . That was only high

school. You survive those things. You don't forget them, but you survive them. And besides, my mother was right. Took me till college to believe it, but I *was* a late bloomer. (*SHE exits and MAN 3 enters.*)

BARRY AUSTIN (MAN 3). Gym class! Anybody remember gym class? You do four hundred push-ups in forty-five seconds or some Neanderthal threatens to shove your jock-strap down your throat, right? And there's always some feeb who can't do anything. We had this kid called Joel the Jelly-Roll, who was like the feeb of all time. Buckowitz, our gym teacher, blew up at him once and told him he was the biggest fuck-up he'd ever seen. Couldn't catch, couldn't throw. He was so fat . . . (*doing a number*) "How fat was he?" He was so fat that when he got benched, nobody else *could* be. Honest! I mean, this guy was so fat that when you saw him in the showers, you couldn't even tell if he had a prick or not. Wanna know how he got his name? One day in the locker room one of the guys says, "Hey, Joel, where's your pecker?" and somebody else says "Here it is!" and holds up this jelly-roll thing from his lunch. So we all start tossing it around, going

Joel, Joel,
Jelly-roll!
Hasn't got a pecker,
So he has to have a hole!
Joel, Joel,
Jelly-roll!

The topper, though, was when Danny shoves the jelly-roll in Joel's face and makes him eat it! I nearly fell over from laughing so hard. Every so often I think of stuff like that and I break up all over again. The wife hates it when I tell that story. (*mimicking her*) "It's not funny, Barry. It's not funny." You hadda be there, y'know? You just hadda be there.

(*As HE goes off a school bell rings. All but MAN 1 enter U.S., dimly lit; THEY are wearing high school clothes and engaged in activities from the past (hallway flirtations, a slow-motion cheerleader routine, etc.). Like the prom dancers earlier in the act, THEY represent an image of former times. MAN 1 enters D.S. and looks at them. As HE turns out and begins to sing "FOR THEM", THEY freeze.*)

MAN 1.
I RAN TO BEAT THE BELL WITH THOSE PEOPLE

EVERY DAY
FOR FOUR YEARS.
RACED AROUND THE TRACK,
MEASURED BACK TO BACK,
LIVED WITH THEM
FOR FOUR YEARS.
YOU SAY GOODBYE AND THEN
YOU GO YOUR SEPARATE WAYS,
BUT TIME AND TIME AGAIN
THERE THEY ARE
IN THE HAZE.

(*The* U.S. *figures come out of their freeze and resume their high
    school activities.*)

SOMETIMES IT'S LIKE THEY'RE WATCHING,
WATCHING AS I GO ON.
DAY OUT, DAY IN
I LOSE, I WIN
AND SOMEHOW I FEEL
I DO IT FOR THEM.

WHY SHOULD I STILL BE BOTHERED?
WHEN WILL THE GHOSTS BE GONE?
HOW CAN I FEEL
MY LIFE IS REAL
WHEN HALF OF THE TIME
I DO IT FOR THEM?

I WONDER, I WONDER . . .

(*The rest of the cast, in a freeze once more, starts singing.
    They're positioned and lit so we can't see them sing; their
    voices represent* MAN 1*'s thoughts.*)

ALL BUT MAN 1.
WHAT WOULD THEY THINK OF ME NOW?
MAN 1.
I WONDER, I WONDER . . .
ALL BUT MAN 1.
HOW WOULD I MEASURE UP NOW?
MAN 1.
I WONDER, I WONDER . . .

ALL BUT MAN 1.
EVEN THOUGH YEARS HAVE GONE BY,
NO MATTER HOW FAR I FLY,
    MAN 1.
WHAT WOULD THEY THINK OF ME?
    ALL.
I WANNA KNOW.
I WANNA KNOW.
I WANNA KNOW.
I WANNA KNOW.

(*Activitity begins again* U.S.)

    MAN 1.
I SOUND LIKE A BROKEN RECORD,
ENDLESSLY SPINNING ON.
RUNNING MY RACE,
MY FOOLISH CHASES,
ONLY TO FIND
I DO IT FOR THEM.
ALWAYS FOR THEM.
LOOKING BACK OVER MY SHOULDER

(*HE looks over his shoulder at the* U.S. *group, now still.*)

    ALL.
FOR THEM.

*   *   *

(*The lights fade out on everyone—MAN 1 last of all. Each of the speeches in the following "revenge sequence" is under-scored. MAN 4 enters as music begins.*)

MAN 4. I'm writing my dissertation on the parameters of social interaction in the American adolescent society. Put most simply, my central thesis is this: that the people who gave me grief in high school oughta be stood up against a wall and have their guts splattered out with a machine gun. (*Music cue. WOMAN 1 enters.*)
WOMAN 1. Rita Morrison once told me that being beautiful was a 24-hour-a-day job, and that sometimes she wished she

could be more "casual" about her appearance . . . the way *I* was. (*Music cue. MAN 2 enters with a yearbook.*)

MAN 2. (*studying the book*) Oh, here he is! Here he is! (*reading*) "Most Outstanding Senior Athlete: Jay Steinhouse." (*HE takes out a pencil and stabs JAY's picture, then rips it. As if dismayed by what he's done:*) Oh! I ripped his head off! (*Music cue. WOMAN 4 enters.*)

WOMAN 4. He's a used-car salesman now—this creep who used to call me Little Miss Tiny Tits. I can't wait to run into him again. He'll say, "What are you doing now?" and I'll say, "I'm teaching at the university." Then I'll say, "And what are *you* doing now?"—and when he tells me he's selling used cars, I'll say, "I'm so glad—that's just where a shit like you belongs!" (*Music cue. MAN 3 enters.*)

MAN 3. I demand an apology from every single person in my class for not recognizing what a great guy I was. What's more, I'm not gonna accept this apology. I demand to know what it's like to walk down the hall in a letter sweater and have everybody smile at you. I demand to be student body president. I demand to be cute. I demand to be awarded a full athletic scholarship to the college of my choice. I demand . . . Aw, hell, I don't want it now—I want it then.

(*Coronation music begins and everyone turns U.S. to applaud, cheer, and throw confetti as WOMAN 3 enters and comes D.S. WOMAN 2, MAN 1, and MAN 5 also rush in to applaud WOMAN 3. The music ends abruptly. The crowd freezes and the light fades out on them as WOMAN 3 begins singing "DIARY OF A HOMECOMING QUEEN". The crowd exits in darkness as she sings.*)

WOMAN 3. (*spoken*) November 30, 1969.

(*sung*)
TODAY I WAS CROWNED THE HOMECOMING QUEEN,
AND JEFF WAS THE FOOTBALL KING.
I WORE MY FLOOR-LENGTH FORMAL
FROM THE JUNIOR PROM LAST SPRING.
BEFORE THE GAME WAS PLAYED
WE LED A BIG PARADE,
AND WE HAD A 50 YARD LINE CORONATION.

ALL THE KIDS WERE CHEERING
AS WE WALKED OUT ON THE FIELD,
AND THERE WERE PEOPLE TAKING PICTURES
EVERYWHERE.

THE STANDS WERE FULL TO BURSTING,
AND THE SENIORS RAISED A BANNER,
AND JEFF POINTED TO OUR NAMES UP IN THE AIR.

THE MARCHING BAND WAS PLAYING,
AND THE KIDS ALL THREW CONFETTI,
AND I FEEL LIKE I STILL HAVE SOME IN MY HAIR.

(*During transitional music SHE moves several steps* D.S.)

(*spoken*) April 16, 1973.

(*sung*)
THE CARPETING CAME, AND SO DID THE RUG
WE BOUGHT FOR THE BEDROOM FLOOR.
JEFF REALLY GOT A BARGAIN
WITH HIS DISCOUNT THROUGH THE STORE.
I LOVE THE WALL TO WALL.
THE BABY HAD A BALL
WHEN THE MEN WERE HERE TO DO THE
    INSTALLATION.

ALL THE KIDS WERE CHEERING
AS WE WALKED OUT ON THE FIELD,
AND THERE WERE PEOPLE TAKING PICTURES
    EVERYWHERE.

THE STANDS WERE FULL TO BURSTING,
AND THE SENIORS RAISED A BANNER,
AND JEFF POINTED TO OUR NAMES UP IN THE AIR.

THE MARCHING BAND WAS PLAYING,
AND THE KIDS ALL THREW CONFETTI,
AND I FEEL LIKE I STILL HAVE SOME IN MY HAIR.

(*SHE again moves* D.S.)

(*spoken*) August 3, 1978

(*sung*)
THIS MORNING I FOUND A NOTE ON THE BED.
IT SAID: "YOU ARE GETTING FAT."
I QUICKLY DRESSED MELINDA,
AND WE FED THE STUPID CAT.
WE CAUGHT A SHOW AT NOON,
A FEATURE-LENGTH CARTOON.
IT'S AMAZING WHAT THEY DO WITH ANIMATION.

(*Chorus music begins again. For a time SHE is unable to sing.*)

THE MARCHING BAND WAS PLAYING,
AND THE KIDS ALL THREW CONFETTI,
AND I FEEL LIKE I STILL HAVE SOME IN MY HAIR.

THE MARCHING BAND WAS PLAYING,
AND THE KIDS ALL THREW CONFETTI,
AND I FEEL LIKE I STILL HAVE SOME IN MY HAIR.

THE MARCHING BAND WAS PLAYING,
AND THE KIDS ALL THREW CONFETTI,
AND I FEEL LIKE I STILL HAVE SOME IN MY HAIR.

I GUESS IT ALWAYS WILL BE THERE.

(*The coronation music begins again. The cheering crowd re-enters, at first in slow motion, and showers her with confetti. All freeze as the music stops abruptly.*)

CURTAIN

ACT TWO

At rise: *The entire cast is once more in the TABLEAU as at the beginning of the play. MAN 4 steps out of it and starts singing "THOUSANDS OF TRUMPETS". The others remain in place.*

MAN 4.
THERE ARE THOUSANDS OF TRUMPETS
IN THOUSANDS OF CLOSETS
THAT NEVER GET PLAYED ANYMORE.
COUNTLESS TRUMPETS IN CASES
IN TUCKED AWAY PLACES
THAT NEVER PARADE ANYMORE.
THERE'S A CLARINET
BACK HOME AT MY MOTHER'S,
IN A CARDBOARD BOX
LIKE THOUSANDS OF OTHERS.
THERE ARE SAXOPHONES,
AND SLIDE TROMBONES
WE PACKED AWAY WAY BACK WHEN;
AND THEY'RE NEVER GONNA SPARKLE IN THE SUN
    AGAIN.

(*One by one the other actors break out of the tableau.*)

MAN 3. I got drawers full of stuff at home I don't know what to do with anymore. Who remembers how to use a slide rule?

WOMAN 4. Isn't it about time I got rid of my notes on the Industrial Revolution?

WOMAN 1. I've still got my baton somewhere, but people tend to be suspicious of a doctor who twirls.

MAN 5. What am I supposed to do with my old protractor?

MAN 2. My copy of *Beowulf*?

WOMAN 2. Tony Green's I.D. bracelet?

MAN 1. That J.V. pennant?

WOMAN 3. My push-up bra?

ALL.
THERE ARE THOUSANDS OF TRUMPETS
IN THOUSANDS OF CLOSETS
THAT NEVER GET PLAYED ANYMORE.
COUNTLESS TRUMPETS IN CASES
IN TUCKED AWAY PLACES

34

THAT NEVER PARADE ANYMORE.
THERE'S A BIG BRASS BAND
OF RUSTY MUSICIANS
THAT AT ONE TIME PLAYED
SOME NOISY RENDITIONS
OF "THE STARS AND STRIPES".
BUT HOLY CRIPES,
IT'S SILENT ALL THROUGH THE LAND;
AND THERE'S NOTHIN' LIKE THE SILENCE
OF A BIG BRASS BAND.
    Man 4.
I WAS THERE.
    All But Man 4.
SO WAS I.
    All.
GOING "RUM BIDDA BUM BUM",
GOD KNOWS WHY.
I WAS THERE;
STEPPING HIGH.
THOSE WERE MY WHITE BUCKS
PROUDLY MARCHING BY
WITH THE BAND.
(*pause*)
WHERE'S THE BAND?
(*pause*)

(*Dance. Tentatively, with much embarrassment, the band re-groups and performs something resembling a high school halftime show. In New York the dance music was played by a pre-recorded marching band. When the dance is fin-ished the song continues.*)

    All.
HALF-TIME IS OVER,
AND SO IS THE THUNDER.
THE FLUTES AND THE FRENCH HORNS
ARE STARTING TO WONDER.
THE BEAT OF THE BASS DRUM,
THE ROLL OF THE SNARE
ARE BUT ECHOES IN THE AIR.
AND THERE ARE THOUSANDS OF TRUMPETS
IN THOUSANDS OF CLOSETS
THAT NEVER GET PLAYED ANYMORE.

COUNTLESS TRUMPETS IN CASES
IN TUCKED AWAY PLACES
THAT NEVER PARADE ANYMORE.
THERE'S A BIG BRASS BAND
OF RUSTY MUSICIANS
THAT AT ONE TIME PLAYED
SOME NOISY RENDITIONS
OF "THE STARS AND STRIPES".
BUT HOLY CRIPES,
IT'S SILENT ALL THROUGH THE LAND;
AND THERE'S NOTHIN' LIKE THE SILENCE
OF A BIG BRASS BAND.

NOTHIN' LIKE A BIG BRASS BAND!

*   *   *

(*After applause, music begins and all but WOMAN 4 parade offstage.*)

GINNY PHILLIPS (WOMAN 4). I like to think I've changed a lot since high school. I mean, I've got a family now, and responsibilities. But then every once in a while somebody says to me something like "You're a real cheerleader type, aren't you?" or "You musta been a cheerleader when you were in school," and I always say, "*Sure* I was!" Maybe some of 'em mean it like a putdown, but that's not the way I take it. I take it as a compliment, like they were saying, "I can see you got a good, positive kind of outlook." O' course then there're the dumbos who think it's a big joke to've been a cheerleader . . . or a big turn-on. One guy even said to me, "I guess you got a lotta practice spreadin' your legs, didn't ya?" Denny—my husband—woulda punched him out in a minute if he heard that. I just turned and walked away. The best fun I ever had was when Molly Baylor and Chrissie Lindell and I did this routine at the state tournament 'cause the Pirates were about ten points behind and everybody was getting real discouraged, and we came out and did "Who's got the muscle?" sixteen times. I mean, we were almost dead at the end. But it really got everybody all charged up, and then when the Pirates came from behind and actually *won*, I felt like I really gave my all and it really *meant* something. People say to me, "Oh, Ginny, you're just too full of pep—I can't keep up with you," but what I hate to see is all the people I know who get so down in the dumps all the time over nothing. You know: worry-worry-worry. Y'know their problem? They don't know how to get *excited* about things. Me, well—ever since my operation I'm just excited to still be alive. When Denny brought me home from the hospital I said, "If we can beat cancer, we can beat anything." And you know what he said to me? He gave me a look like who-is-this-crazy-woman-I'm-married-to? and said, "You really *are* a cheerleader, aren't you?"

(*SHE exits and WOMEN 1, 2 and 3 and MEN 2 and 3 enter. This sequence is underscored.*)

MAN 2. Of the 648 kids in my class, there are only four or five I still keep in touch with. But sometimes I can't help wondering about the others. Bet Joey Lambert's voice never *did* change.

WOMAN 2. What ever happened to Eric Rice, who told me that the human brain stops functioning at age 30?

WOMAN 3. I heard last week that Donna Sullivan passed her bar exam. Donna Sullivan! I used to help her with her homework.

MAN 3. Jerry Davis, Charlie Silverman—I know what happened to them. They went to Nam and they didn't come back. Hell, I can still see 'em sittin' around the pizza place with the rest of us, talkin' about what we were gonna be.

(*WOMEN 2 and 3 and MEN 2 and 3 exit together, and underscoring ends as WOMAN 1 starts to speak.*)

WOMAN 1. I always wondered what happened to Johnny— Johnny DeBernardis. He wasn't a real close friend of mine, but I adored him. The thing I always think of is the time he came into Social Studies with his face painted blue, and Mr. Reikle got all upset and told him to wash his face or he'd be sent home. Johnny just said, "Am I to understand, Mr. Reikle, that you're discriminating against me because of my color?" Well, we all started to laugh because we knew Mr. Reikle was a bigot, but nobody'd ever challenged him like that before. Reikle began sort of sputtering, and then he said we were all human garbage—that's what he said, honest!—and he just walked out of the classroom and never came back. I *adored* Johnny DeBernardis.

(*MAN 5 enters and speaks to the audience. WOMAN 1 listens to him.*)

MAN 5. Johnny D. was my year, but in some ways he was like ten years ahead of me. He saw through all the crap before I knew it *was* crap. But that meant the administration really came down on him. If they could, they woulda crucified him. Johnny just laughed in their faces, and somehow he always got away with it.

(*MAN 4 enters; WOMAN 1 and MAN 5 listen to him.*)

MAN 4. I remember when Johnny set up a stand to sell bricks in center hall. He had this sign that said, "SHOW YOUR SCHOOL SPIRIT—BUY A BRICK." They came with a mimeographed sheet that said things like "Why'd you buy this brick, anyway? What are you gonna do with it? Why do you think school spirit is so important?" He was weird, that's for sure. I still got my brick somewhere. And y'know what? I miss that crazy son of a bitch.

(*MAN 1 enters; WOMAN 1, MAN 4 and MAN 5 listen to him.*)

MAN 1. Johnny DeBernardis was a pain in the ass. He thought he was so smart, but all he did was make a fool of himself. I guess he was what you'd call a radical. If you ask me, he was only a short little bastard with bad acne who needed a haircut.
MAN 4. He was crazy, really crazy. (*MAN 4 exits on this line.*)
MAN 5. Y'know how they always told you in school to stand up for what you believe, and then if you did they'd kill you? Well, they couldn't kill Johnny. (*MAN 5 exits.*)
MAN 1. Guys like that can't hack it in the real world. They just can't hack it. Probably turned out to be a druggie and burned his brains out on LSD. (*MAN 1 exits.*)
WOMAN 1. When Sally told me what happened to him I couldn't believe it. I thought he'd be a lawyer or go into politics or . . . I don't know. The last thing I ever expected him to be was a high school teacher. But when you think about it, that's exactly what he oughta be. (*WOMAN 1 exits.*)

(*Reunion intro music begins. We see WOMAN 3 holding her reunion announcement and studying it in a state of shock. SHE reads aloud.*)

WOMAN 3. "Hear ye! Hear ye! Our long-awaited tenth reunion will be held at Robert Louis Stevenson High . . ."

(*Music continues under as the other actors appear with their announcements in hand. Their reading of them is slightly overlapped.*)

MAN 1. "The class of '71 from Southside High is cordially invited to attend . . ."
MAN 4. "It's reunion time!"
MAN 3. Twenty years?

(*WOMAN 2 looks at her announcement in silence, then crumples it up.*)

WOMAN 4. "Time to say hello again to all your friends from Floral Park's Class of '67."
WOMAN 1. "Remember the good old days at Harris High . . ."
MAN 5. "Come as you are and meet the folks who remember you the way you were."

(*WOMAN 2 uncrumples her announcement and studies it.*)
MAN 2.
THERE HE GOES AGAIN,
ALL BUT MAN 2.
HE'S/SHE'S THERE AGAIN.
MAN 2.
HUMMIN' HIS SONGS.
ALL BUT MAN 2.
SINGIN' "COME ALONG, COME ON AND COME ALONG,"
MAN 2.
HE'S THERE AGAIN
ALL BUT MAN 2.
"COME ALONG FOR THE RIDE."
ALL.
SINGIN' "COME ALONG."

(*Music continues under as everyone makes preparations for and starts toward his reunion. The scene changes to represent a composite of several reunion locales. The cast enters, looks around, then stands motionless and sings.*)

ALL.
SO HERE WE ARE
  MAN 1. I knew I shouldn't have come. I knew it.
  ALL.
PINNING ON OUR NAMETAGS.
  MAN 5. Hey — what happened to their hair?
  ALL.
FLASHING BACK ON SCHOOL,
ACTING CALM AND COOL,
SCARED AS EVER.
HERE WE ARE.
  WOMAN 3. If I keep sweating like this, I'm going home.
  ALL.
WE SCAN THE ROOM,
WE CATCH OUR BREATH,
THE HEARTBEAT RACES.
GUESS IT'S NOW OR NEVER.
FACE THE CLASS;
FAIL OR PASS.
GOD, IT'S BEEN FOREVER!
IT'S BEEN FOREVER.
HERE WE ARE.

(*Underscoring begins and continues under all the scenes in the
    following "reunion sequence" except where designated
    otherwise. This underscoring is intended to be the kind of
    innocuous background music one hears at a reunion.*
*The sequence is a montage of many different reunions. We are
    not in one particular place with one particular class but con-
    stantly shifting, regrouping, witnessing first one encounter
    here, then another someplace else. The actors change
    character from scene to scene.*
*Between scenes there are brief musical swells and/or bursts of
    laughter, greetings, conversation and activity which then
    subside as the next scene begins.*)

  MAN 3. Hey, beanbrain!
  MAN 4. Corey! You old douchebag!
  MAN 3. What the hell are you doing now?
  MAN 4. Me? I'm a doctor.
  MAN 3. Aw, come off it.
  MAN 4. No, really. I'm in the neurosurgery unit up at the
medical center.

IS THERE LIFE AFTER HIGH SCHOOL?   41

Man 3. Neurosurgery? Holy shit. Last time I saw you, you were the Wild Man of Wagner High.

* * *

Woman 3. That's Peggy Carstairs. She sat next to me in Home Ec. And that's Warren Daniels. He's the guy who threw up on me in the cafeteria. And there's Madge Piercy . . .

Man 1. Aren't you gonna talk to anybody?

Woman 3. Not to *them*. Far as I can see the only people who came are the real drips. Wait a minute! That's Tony Pulaski!

Man 1. Well, at least there's somebody you can talk to.

Woman 3. Are you kidding? Tony Pulaski was Student Body President. Why would he wanna talk to *me*?

* * *

(*WOMAN 4 takes a photo of MEN 2, 3 and 5.*)

Woman 4. Hold it! That's perfect!

* * *

Woman 2. I'm just so glad you're divorced!

Woman 1. *You're* glad.

Woman 2. I didn't want to be the only one. I almost didn't come tonight because I couldn't face everybody saying, "Hey— where's Eddie?"

Woman 1. I forgot. You and Eddie were voted Cutest Couple, right?

Woman 2. You got it. Cutest Couple ever to get married too young.

Woman 1. Come on, cheer up. Donald Wilson just told me you look sensational.

Woman 2. Really? Donald Wilson?

Woman 1. Uh-huh. And what's more, *he's* divorced, too.

* * *

Man 2. Steskel's class. You sat up front.

Woman 4. Sure. Oh, sure.

Man 2. Never forget that guy.

Woman 4. Who?

MAN 2. Steskel.

WOMAN 4. Oh, me neither. Excuse me. Some friends of mine are holding a table for me, and I promised I'd sit with them. (*Underscoring concludes.*)

MAN 2. Oh. Well, maybe I could . . .?

WOMAN 4. Hm?

MAN 2. Join you?

WOMAN 4. Well, we . . . I mean . . . There are lots of tables.

(*Everyone on stage except MAN 2 freezes at this point. HE sings "HIGH SCHOOL ALL OVER AGAIN". The entire company comes briefly to life during the interjected lines.*)

MAN 2.
HIGH SCHOOL ALL OVER AGAIN,
THE OLD FUN AND GAMES.
HIGH SCHOOL, PLAYED OUT AT A TABLE FOR TEN.

MAN 1. (*to WOMAN 4, about MAN 2*) He's not gonna sit with *us*, is he?

MAN 2.
I KNOW, THE GUYS ARE IN TIES,
AND THE GIRLS HAVE NEW NAMES,
BUT IT'S HIGH SCHOOL ALL OVER AGAIN.

MAN 3. (*calling to a woman*) Hey, stuck-up! (*All the women turn toward him.*)

MAN 2.
COME BACK, COME BACK TO THE LAND
OF THE KINGS AND THE QUEENS.
COME BACK, IF ONLY TO SEE HOW YOU SCORE.

MAN 4. (*to WOMAN 2, about MAN 2*) Do you believe those shoes he's wearing?

MAN 2.
IT'S TIME FOR DOIN' A FEW
O' YOUR FAVORITE ROUTINES.
YES, IT'S JUST LIKE THOSE OLD DAYS OF YORE.

(*WOMEN 2, 3 and 4 scream with pleasure as they catch sight of each other.*)

MAN 2.
I THINK I'VE SEEN THIS FLICK BEFORE.

(*WOMEN 2, 3 and 4 go through an old cheerleader routine. This short scene is not underscored.*)

WOMEN 2, 3 and 4. We're the kids from Carey High.
We never put out
And we never get high! (*WOMAN 1 comes running over to them.*)
    WOMAN 1. C'mon! Do it right! Do it right!
    WOMEN 2, 3 and 4. Aw, Cindy!
    WOMEN 1, 2, 3 and 4. We're the kids from Carey High.
We never give up
And we never say die!
    WOMAN 1. Well, that's better! (*All freeze again as MAN 2 resumes singing.*)
    MAN 2.
HIGH SCHOOL ALL OVER AGAIN.
THE BEAST WILL NOT DIE.
WE GOT OLD CHEERLEADERS DOIN' OLD CHEERS.
    WOMEN 1, 2, 3 and 4. Yay, team!
    MAN 2.
JUST WHEN YOU THOUGHT YOU WERE SAFE,
HIGH SCHOOL SAYS "HI".
YOU FORGET WHERE YOU'VE BEEN ALL THESE
    YEARS,
WHEN HIGH SCHOOL APPEARS.

(*The cast breaks from the freeze and MEN 1, 3, 4 and 5 start playing football with a shoe. There is no underscoring here.*)

    MAN 3. 38, 17, 52—hike! (*receiving the shoe*) Hey, Terry! It's your pass!
    MAN 1. Mine? Okay! (*MAN 3 throws the shoe and MAN 1 catches it.*)
    MEN 3 & 4. Yay!!
    MAN 5. Way to go!
    MAN 1. I'm in better shape *now*.
    MAN 4. Keep practicing, Terry. Maybe someday you'll make the first string.

(*Everyone begins singing.*)

ALL BUT MAN 2.
WELCOME BACK
MAN 2.
RAH RAH RAH
ALL BUT MAN 2.
WELCOME BACK
TO THE HIGH AND THE LOW.
MAN 2.
SAME OLD TUNE
ALL BUT MAN 2.
LA LA LA
MAN 2.
SAME OLD TUNE
WE ALL SANG LONG AGO.

HURRY ON DOWN,
DON'T PUT UP A FIGHT.
HEY, COME MEET THE HUSBANDS AND WIVES.
SAY, WHAT DO YOU KNOW,
THEY GOT RERUNS TONIGHT
OF THE HAPPIEST YEARS OF OUR LIVES.
ALL BUT MAN 2.
HIGH SCHOOL . . .
MAN 2.
I GOT THE FEELIN' I'VE BEEN HERE BEFORE.
ALL BUT MAN 2
ALL OVER AGAIN!
HIGH SCHOOL . . .
MAN 2.
I GOT THE FEELIN' I'VE BEEN HERE BEFORE.
ALL BUT MAN 2.
ALL OVER AGAIN!
HIGH SCHOOL . . .
MAN 2.
GOT THE FEELIN' I'VE BEEN HERE BEFORE.
ALL BUT MAN 2.
ALL OVER AGAIN!
HIGH SCHOOL!
MAN 2.
I BEEN HERE BEFORE.

*   *   *

(*After applause the underscoring resumes. MAN 3 takes a photo of WOMAN 1 and MAN 4, then WOMAN 4 comes over to join them.*)

MAN 4. (*to WOMAN 1*) And this is Erica, the woman I'm living with.

WOMAN 1. Oh!

WOMAN 4. We're engaged. Ray makes it sound as if . . .

WOMAN 1. (*breaking in*) I understand. I'm old-fashioned myself.

MAN 4. (*to Woman 4*) Judy and I go back a long way. We started dating at what? Fifteen?

WOMAN 1. Fourteen. He was the first boy I ever dated. I'll tell you a secret even he doesn't know: he was the first boy I ever kissed.

WOMAN 4. (*at a loss*) Well, that's certainly . . .

MAN 4. Sure was a long time ago.

WOMAN 1. We went to all the dances together.

WOMAN 4. (*to MAN 4*) Really? You used to dance?

WOMAN 1. Oh, doesn't he still? He was terrific.

MAN 4. I had a terrific partner.

WOMAN 1. Honestly, Ray—you don't dance anymore?

MAN 4. Not really, no.

WOMAN 4. We have other interests.

WOMAN 1. Well, sure. I'm sure you do. (*to MAN 4, after a brief awkward pause*) Listen—say hi to your sister for me.

MAN 4. Sure.

WOMAN 1. (*to WOMAN 4*) And get him out on the dance floor sometime, okay?

* * *

MAN 3. (*with a laugh*) Whaddaya mean, make-out artist?

MAN 1. If you weren't, who was?

MAN 3. I'm not saying I didn't get to first base a couple o' times, but I sure don't remember any home runs.

MAN 1. That's not what you said back then. Remember the old parking spot on Adams Road?

MAN 3. Remember it? I was there last week—with Peggy.

MAN 1. Your wife? You took your wife?

MAN 3. What can I tell ya? I got this crazy idea. Lucky for me she's just as crazy as I am. We got the kids to bed early, and I put on some English Leather. It was pitch black except for the moon, and we started necking. Then I said, "Hey! Did you ever do it in a car?" She turned real serious all of a sudden and said, "I'm not the kind of person who does that sort of thing." We looked at each other and started to laugh. Here we are, married eleven years, with three kids at home, and I finally find out just where she draws the line.

* * *

MAN 5. I always thought you'd go into modeling or something.

WOMAN 2. I did for a while, but . . .

MAN 5. Nobody's getting any younger, I guess.

WOMAN 2. It's not really a steady business.

(*Underscoring concludes.*)

MAN 5. Heard that. Like the suit?

WOMAN 2. Mm-hm.

MAN 5. Brooks Brothers.

WOMAN 2. Great!

MAN 5. Got it in Hong Kong.

WOMAN 2. A Brooks Brothers suit?

MAN 5. They're cheaper over there. Not that money's an object.

WOMAN 2. Yeah.

MAN 5. You been to Hong Kong?

WOMAN 2. No.

MAN 5. Europe?

WOMAN 2. Uh-uh.

MAN 5. Well, you got time, right? Never can tell when things'll start to break for you. But jeez, you used to be something, y'know? You really used to be something.

* * *

(*The party noises die down. WOMAN 3 and WOMAN 4 see each other across the stage as music begins. THEY start toward each other and on coming together turn toward the audience. They sing "FRAN AND JANIE" side by side, looking at each other only where specified.*)

Both.
WE DON'T KNOW WHERE TO START.
AND SO WE SAY "HOW LONG HAS IT BEEN?"
WE JOKE ABOUT OUR AGE,
AND HOW THE YEARS JUST FLEW.
WE SAY WE MEANT TO WRITE,
AS OLD FRIENDS ALWAYS DO.
   Fran. (*WOMAN 4 to WOMAN 3*)
AND ARE YOU STILL TOO SMART?
   Janie. (*WOMAN 3 to WOMAN 4*)
AND DO YOU STILL MIX BOURBON WITH GIN?
   Both. (*to each other*)
AND DID YOU SEE THE WORLD?
AND DID YOU MEET A MAN?

(*THEY gradually turn out and face front.*)

   Both.
AND DID YOU FALL IN LOVE,
THE WAY WE USED TO PLAN,
BEFORE OUR LIVES BEGAN?
REMEMBER—
FRAN AND JANIE
SHARING SECRETS,
SWAPPING DAYDREAMS,
DROPPING BY.
FRAN AND JANIE
SHARING HEARTBREAKS,
SHOUTING WISHES
AT THE SKY.
PLAYING RECORDS,
SLEEPING OVER,
TALKING GIRL-TALK,
YOU REMEMBER.
   Janie.
FRAN AND JANIE,
   Fran.
FRAN AND JANIE,
   Both.
LIKE A SINGLE WORD.
(*to each other*)
SO TELL US HOW YOU ARE.

SO HOW'S YOUR LIFE SO FAR?
SO DID YOU CATCH THAT STAR?
(*facing front*)
TWO OLD FRIENDS,
ALL GROWN UP.
ONE IS SINGLE,
AND ONE HAS A COUPLE O' KIDS
   Fran. (*to JANIE*)
AND A HUSBAND NAMED BOB.
   Janie. (*to FRAN*)
AND A CHANCE FOR THIS JOB.
   Fran. (*to JANIE*)
TAKING COURSES AT NIGHT.
   Janie. (*to FRAN*)
COMING OFF A ROMANCE.
   Both. (*facing front*)
A MILLION FACTS
AND FEELINGS TO SORT.
TWO OLD FRIENDS
WITH MUCH TO REPORT,
WHO NEVER *DID* KNOW HOW
TO MAKE LONG STORIES SHORT.

SO WE TALK 'TIL WE LAUGH
AND WE LAUGH 'TIL WE CRY.
AND WE GO ON AND ON,
MY GIRL FRIEND AND I.

(*THEY clasp hands but remain facing front.*)

   Both.
FRAN AND JANIE
SHARING SECRETS,
PASSING BY.
FRAN AND JANIE
SHOUTING WISHES
AT THE SKY.
AND BEHIND US,
FRAN AND JANIE
CALLING BOYS UP,
PAINTING POSTERS,
BUILDING SNOWMEN,

LOOKING FORWARD,
YOU AND I,
(*to each other*)
TO THE PRESENT DAY.

(*slowly letting go of each other's hands and facing front*)

WE TALK OF WHAT'S IN STORE
AS WE'VE TALKED BEFORE,
UNTIL THERE'S NOTHING MORE
TO SAY.

(*THEY turn to each other, then embrace on the last chord.*)

*   *   *

(*Underscoring resumes after applause.*)

MAN 1. (*showing photographs*) This is Chrissie and Jennie and Jim Junior. That's Ellie holding Jennie.
WOMAN 1. She's so pretty!
MAN 1. Who?
WOMAN 1. Your wife.
MAN 1. Oh, right. Right!

*   *   *

(*MAN 5, who has been standing apart from the others, drinking, is approached by MAN 4.*)

MAN 4. Hi. I'm Ed Kendall.
MAN 5. So?
MAN 4. I just thought . . . You were in my class, weren't you?
MAN 5. Oh yeah. Your class. Your year. Your school. I was there.
MAN 4. (*peering at his nametag*) I don't remember . . .
MAN 5. (*breaking in*) Why would you? Only time you ever said "hi" to me before was when you wanted my vote. So what can I do for you? You still running for class president?
MAN 4. Look, pal. I don't know what your problem is.
MAN 5. (*raising his voice*) I don't go for All-American ass-holes, that's my problem.

(*Underscoring stops abruptly. MAN 5's wife (WOMAN 3) hurries over to him.*)

MAN 5. You wanna make something of it?
WOMAN 3. Larry, come on.
MAN 5. Look—maybe he wants to make something of it.
MAN 4. I don't. I really don't.
MAN 5. See! Look at 'im back off. Whatsa matter? So you were a big deal. So what?
WOMAN 3. Larry, come on. Please?
MAN 5. (*lashing out*) That was high school! High school!
WOMAN 3. Larry, for God's sake.
MAN 4. Cool it, okay?
MAN 5. Cool it, shit! You always looked down your nose at guys like me, didn't you?
MAN 4. No, I . . .
MAN 5. You and your hot-shit crowd with your hot-shit girlfriends. I woulda liked ta been the one who stuck it to Beverly Naylor prom night, I'm tellin' ya.
WOMAN 3. Larry, shut up. We're going home.
MAN 5. Sure—why not? Just wanted to tell him what I think of him. (*yelling*) Nothing! That's what I think! Nothing!
WOMAN 3. (*to MAN 4, as she and her husband leave*) I'm sorry. I'm sorry. (*THEY exit and re-enter later as different characters.*)

*   *   *

(*The underscoring begins again. It is the prom music from Act I. MAN 2 and MAN 3 are watching WOMAN 4, who's dancing with MAN 1.*)

MAN 3. I'd ask her to dance, but . . .
MAN 2. But what?
MAN 3. Hell, she's not gonna say yes. She isn't even gonna say maybe.
MAN 2. How do you know?
MAN 3. She never gave me the time of day.
MAN 2. Go on, go on! Look: she's on her own.

(*The two of them look to see that the man she's been dancing with has left. MAN 3 hesitates, then goes over to her.*)

MAN 3. Excuse me, but . . .

WOMAN 4. Steven!

MAN 3. You remember?

WOMAN 4. Of course.

MAN 3. I'm just drunk enough to ask you to dance.

WOMAN 4. (*smiling*) But not too drunk to dance?

MAN 3. Nope. (*THEY start dancing together.*)

WOMAN 4. Still don't talk much.

MAN 3. Hm?

WOMAN 4. You were always like that. I had this great crush on you junior year, and you couldn't've ever said more than three words to me.

MAN 3. *You* had a crush on *me*? (*HE stops dancing, amazed.*)

WOMAN 4. Uh-huh. What's the matter? Steven . . .?

(*HE beams at her, shakes his head, and they dance off. The prom underscoring ends.*)

*   *   *

(*MAN 2, looking at a yearbook, exclaims to MAN 4.*)

MAN 2. Oh man! you gotta see this to believe it!

*   *   *

(*WOMAN 2 and MAN 1 observe the others from across the room.*)

WOMAN 2. So these are the kids I went to school with. Whaddaya think?

MAN 1. I think you should have been voted sexiest.

WOMAN 2. Well, thank God for that. (*points out another woman*) See that girl? (*Music begins.*)

MAN 1. Uh-huh.

WOMAN 2. She's who I wanted to be. She was so pretty and popular and poised.

MAN 1. Wait a minute! That's how I always figured you must've been.

WOMAN 2. No way. But I almost died trying. (*SHE begins singing "I'M GLAD YOU DIDN'T KNOW ME".*)

WOMAN 2.
I CAN JUST SEE ME AT SIX AND SEVENTEEN,
TYPICAL DOWN TO MY CIRCLE PIN.
PIERCING MY EARS WITH THE FUTURE NURSES CLUB,
WORKING LIKE MAD TO BE "IN".

I'M SO GLAD YOU DIDN'T KNOW ME.
WHAT A NOTHING I WAS THEN.
I'M JUST GLAD YOU DIDN'T KNOW ME.
I'M GLAD YOU DIDN'T KNOW ME WHEN.

MAN 1.
I'M THANKFUL TOO
THAT I DIDN'T KNOW YOU,
'CAUSE THAT WOULD'VE MEANT YOU KNEW ME.
SINGING MY FOLK SONGS,
OR LEARNING TO SMOKE,
OR PANICKED AT PULLING A "D".
AND SPEAKING OF FEARS,
I HAD AN ERECTION
THE WHOLE FOUR YEARS.

WOMAN 2. (*spoken*) No kidding!
MAN 1.
I'M SO GLAD YOU DIDN'T KNOW ME.
I WASN'T READY FOR YOU THEN.
WOMAN 2. (*spoken*) Sounds like you were.
MAN 1.
I'M JUST GLAD YOU DIDN'T KNOW ME.
THANK GOD YOU DIDN'T KNOW ME . . .
WOMAN 2.
PICTURE ME PEPPY, BUT FAKE AS THEY COME,
MAKING CORSAGES OF JUICY FRUIT GUM.
MAN 1.
PICTURE A GEEK ON THE EDGE OF HIS CHAIR,
WAVING HIS HAND IN THE AIR:
(*spoken*) "Ooh, call on me! Call on me!"
WOMAN 2.
PICTURE A PHONY,
MAN 1.
PICTURE HOW SUAVE I COULD BE,
WOMAN 2.
DOIN' THE PONY.

Man 1.

PASSING MY BROTHER'S I.D.

  Woman 2.

I WAS THE WORST.

  Man 1.

AND I WAS AS BAD.

  Both.

PICTURE THE DATES WE'DA HAD!

  Woman 2.

I'M GLAD YOU DIDN'T KNOW ME

  Man 1.

I'M GLAD . . .

GLAD THAT YOU WEREN'T AROUND.

  Woman 2.

AT EISENHOWER HIGH.

  Man 1.

WHAT A CREEP YOU'DA FOUND.

  Woman 2.

AMEN,

  Both.

GOOD RIDDANCE, 'N GOODBYE!

GOODBYE!

HAND ME NO YEARBOOKS TO SIGN.

AND DON'T EVER ASK TO SEE MINE.

I WANT NO AULD LANG SYNE.

I'M GLAD YOU DIDN'T KNOW ME.

GLAD YOU DIDN'T KNOW ME WHEN.

'CAUSE IF YOU HAD GONE TO *MY* SCHOOL

WE'D'VE NEVER HAD A PRAYER.

YOU'D'VE HATED ME IN HIGH SCHOOL.

I'M GLAD YOU WEREN'T THERE.

  Man 1.

PASSING ON THE STAIR.

  Woman 2.

PASSING ON THE STAIR.

  Both.

GLAD YOU DIDN'T KNOW ME . . .

  Woman 2.

SAVING ALL THE SEATS.

MAN 1.
CLOWNING IN THE BLEACHERS.
WOMAN 2.
PRESSING ALL THE PLEATS.
MAN 1.
BROWNING UP THE TEACHERS.
BOTH.
PUSHING ALL THE WAY
TO GRADUATION DAY!

*   *   *

(*WOMEN 1 and 3 and MAN 5 are exchanging phone numbers.*)

MAN 5. 247-3115.

(*Underscoring resumes.*)

WOMAN 1. (*as she writes it down*) . . . 3115. I'm practically blind without my glasses, but I'd be damned if I was gonna wear them tonight.

WOMAN 3. Here's my business card.

WOMAN 1. Your business card! I forgot we all grew up.

MAN 5. I didn't grow up. I just got older.

WOMAN 1. Let's not use that word, okay?

MAN 5. Y'know, it's funny . . . I didn't come to the first re-union 'cause I felt I hadn't changed enough.

WOMAN 3. I know the feeling.

MAN 5. Second time around I thought, "How can I go back if I'm not rich and famous?"

WOMAN 1. Or married.

WOMAN 3. Or glamorous.

MAN 5. But when I got the announcement this time I thought, "What the hell?". The worst thing about high school was think-ing you were in some kind of contest all the time. But I mean, what's the contest? All I know is, I wouldn't have missed seeing you guys again for anything.

(*These three embrace as the rest of the cast is saying goodbye to each other, then separate. Everyone begins singing.*)

ALL.
TIME HAS COME.

THE NIGHT IS WINDING DOWN,
WINDING DOWN.
TIME TO CLOSE THE BAR.
TIME TO GET THE CAR.
TIME HAS FLOWN.

(*They remove their nametags as they sing.*)

AND ONCE AGAIN
HERE WE ARE.
HERE WE ARE.
HERE WE ARE.
ENEMIES AND FRIENDS,
ALL THE ODDS AND ENDS
OF ANOTHER TIME.

(*By the time the singing ends, the reunion scenery has disappeared. Music continues under as each actor echoes a line heard earlier in the play.*)

WOMAN 3. And I remember thinking I could die happy now.

MAN 5. I never said I give, that's the thing. I wouldn't.

WOMAN 2. I still remember exactly what I wore on Elimination Day.

MAN 1. This was my one chance, and I only had a second to decide.

MAN 2. Hearing that guy yell my name has gotta be one of the best moments in my whole life.

WOMAN 1. Miss Haskell just kept saying "Is it true?" "Is it true?" "Is it true?"

WOMAN 4. You really *are* a cheerleader, aren't you?

MAN 3. You hadda be there, you know? You just hadda be there.

(*As each speaks, HE or SHE moves to a spot on stage from which HE can easily step into the TABLEAU which began both acts of the play.*
Music ends as MAN 4 begins speaking. Lights dim on the others.)

JOEL NYQUIST (MAN 4). I drove by my old school this afternoon, and I stopped for a while to watch the kids playing baseball on South Field. They seemed so young! — hardly like high school kids at all. I'd been watching for maybe five minutes before I realized that the old guy who was coaching the team was Mr. Buckowitz, my Phys. Ed. teacher from way back in freshman year. Back then I was fat, real fat, and about a foot shorter than I am now. The guys used to call me Joel the Jelly-Roll. Mr. Buckowitz told the class one time that I was the most uncoordinated kid he'd ever had in all his years of gym-teaching. I went home that day and got a razor blade out of the medicine cabinet and sat on the side of the bathtub for three hours. I remember thinking, "I can't even kill myself," and I could just hear Buckowitz and all the others laughing. But there he was! — today, on South Field, and I wanted to hate him again the way I'd hated him when I was fourteen. I wanted to walk up to him and say, "I know what you are. Don't think I've forgotten what you did to me." But he was this little man — so much smaller than I remembered him, and so much older. He must be about ready to retire now. And besides — I don't hate him anymore. I don't have to. I'm not fourteen, and I don't have to obey him, and I'm not Joel the Jelly-Roll anymore. Jesus Christ! Sometimes when I look back, all I can think is: I made it! I made it! I made it!

(*Music plays as MAN 4 and the rest of the cast step into the opening TABLEAU, as if posing for a class picture.*)

CURTAIN

PROPERTY LIST

p. 14 yearbooks (2, each from a different school)
p. 21 briefcases (2)
p. 24 American flag
p. 28 schoolbooks, notebooks, pompoms, shoulder pads and other assorted high school paraphernalia for Upstage figures
p. 31 yearbook, pencil, confetti
p. 38 reunion announcements (9, varied)
p. 39 nametags (9, varied), punch cups, punch bowl
p. 41 camera with flash
p. 43 shoe
p. 45 camera
p. 49 wallet with photos
p. 51 yearbook
p. 54 address books, pens, business card

SOUND CUES

p. 7   school bell, roll call
p. 28 school bell
p. 35 marching band

57

NEW BROADWAY DRAMAS
from
SAMUEL FRENCH, INC.

AMADEUS – AMERICAN BUFFALO – BENT – COLD STORAGE – COME BACK TO THE 5 & DIME, JIMMY DEAN, JIMMY DEAN – COMEDIANS – THE CRUCIFER OF BLOOD – THE CURSE OF AN ACHING HEART – DO YOU TURN SOMERSAULTS? – THE DRESSER – DUET FOR ONE – EMINENT DOMAIN – FAITH HEALER – THE GIN GAME – HEARTLAND – I WON'T DANCE – KNOCKOUT – A LESSON FROM ALOES – NED AND JACK – NUTS – PAST TENSE – SCENES AND REVELATIONS – THE SHADOW BOX – THE SUICIDE – TO GRANDMOTHER'S HOUSE WE GO – THE WATER ENGINE – WINGS

For descriptions of plays, consult our free Basic Catalogue of Plays.

HOME-BUILT

Lighting Equipment

for The Small Stage
By THEODORE FUCHS

This volume presents a series of fourteen simplified designs for building various types of stage lighting and control equipment, with but one purpose in mind—to enable the amateur producer to acquire a complete set of stage lighting equipment at the lowest possible cost. The volume is 8½" x 11" in size, with heavy paper and spiral binding—features which make the volume well suited to practical workshop use.

Community Theatre

A MANUAL FOR SUCCESS
By JOHN WRAY YOUNG

The ideal text for anyone interested in participating in Community Theatre as a vocation or avocation. "Organizing a Community Theatre," "A Flight Plan for the Early Years," "Programming for People—Not Computers," and other chapters are blueprints for solid growth. "Technical, Business and Legal Procedures" cuts a safe and solvent path through some tricky undergrowth. Essential to the library of all community theatres, and to the schools who will supply them with talent in the years to come.